The Soil That Raised Me

The Soil That Raised Me

Roger Watters

ONION
RIVER
PRESS

Onion River Press
89 Church Street
Burlington, VT 05401

info@onionriverpress.com
www.onionriverpress.com

ISBN: 978-1-966607-11-3
Library of Congress Control Number: 2025912535

Contents

PART I

Refreshed

The playful screams
are flowing from
the sledding hill,
but not from the little
girl seated up front.

She is being introduced
to the joys of sledding
by her preschool teacher
whose childhood memories
are being refreshed.

Assembled

The license plates indicate the
distance traveled to arrive at
this small church in the woods,

a setting fondly remembered
by the family when they
used to live in this area.

All are now assembled to
recognize the life of their
father, partner, and friend.

The memories left behind
with each of them will
always be theirs to cherish.

Arctic Blast

The sound of the wind

traveling across the

broad lake resembles

that of a freight train

which has no station.

Solution

The recent wet snowfall
sits on top of the evergreen
bushes like a tabletop.

With freezing temperatures,
it didn't take long for the
squirrels to discover their

new access point to the feeder.
Might as well spread some seed on
nature's table so everyone can eat.

Fading Light

The fire is dwindling.
Why? She loves the kids
but for some reason,
the light is fading.

She needs more for
herself, but what?
Luckily, there are options.
Still, leaving will be hard.

Rare Display

The northern arctic wind
causes slender whirlpools
to rise off the open water
high into the frigid air.

The rare display inspires people
to stand in the brutal wind
along a frozen shoreline
with cameras ready to record—

before the whirlpools lose
their source of fuel when they reach the
frozen bays or shore, where
they'll silently vanish from view.

Gullible Me

Squirrel proof,

the tag said.

Gullible me,

I bought it.

Now we watch

the squirrels

feed upside down

from the bird feeder.

What We Know

Is the sun going to shine?
Are we supposed to get snow?
How many people are coming?
We plan by what we know.

We tend to put off planning for
things that make us uncomfortable.
When tomorrow becomes today,
we resolve that in some way.

As family arrives, you'll
refresh shared memories.
Laughter—and yes, tears—will flow
because of what we know.

For Leslie
Keep Smiling

Layers

We arrive at the restaurant to
celebrate the date of my birth
near a gentle, layered waterfall.

With the daylight fading,
it's not hard to observe how
the ice has restricted the flow.

The various levels highlight
the stone formations that
form the gradual falls.

With light conversation,
our minds drift away like
the water passing by.

Each rocky layer
symbolizes a phase of my
life so vividly for me.

As the light fades, so does
our view when we hear
Happy Birthday being sung.

A young woman was also
celebrating; we shared
birthday wishes with her.

I don't know how many
layers of my life are left but
I look forward to the next.

Early Evening

The early evening sky
unveils a translucent figure—
a full moon not quite
prepared for exposure.

As the sky darkens,
the boldness we're used to
develops along with a
supporting cast.

Occupants ready to take
their positional review as
the earth silently rotates
to compliment the night.

In and Out

The first goose of the year
flies over from the lake.

Where does it go now that
it's alone, at this time of year?

Heavy snow predicted this week;
bird feeders have been busy.

Squirrels arrive with the light,
then take turns at the feeders.

If there's an opening, the birds behave
like bees at a hive, flying in and out.

The Door

The fire trucks rest
in front of the school.

The honor guard will be
just inside for the funeral.

Apprehension sets in
as I get closer to the door.

If I open the door,
will I walk into the past?

How will the past react?
I've been away so long.

As the door opens
smiles greet me, along

with heartfelt handshakes—
a genuine welcome.

My uneasiness is replaced with
gratitude for opening the door.

Faces Like Mine

As I enter the auditorium
for the funeral, I see familiar
faces that have aged.

Why are there just
a few faces like
mine looking back?

They are trying to figure
out who I am, just like I am
attempting to do with them.

Smiles evolve when that
feat is accomplished
with a wave of the hand.

The current status of
all in attendance has
been uniquely updated.

It's Official

It's late March, and
the weather has been perfect
for making maple syrup.

Few warm weather
guests had arrived
until last night.

A flock flew in under
the guise of darkness,
as if we wouldn't notice.

Morning light barely discolors
the darkness when the
first calls awaken us:

The robins have arrived.
Dig out the gardening tools—
spring is officially here.

Spring Flowers

The last of the snow has faded away.

Green tips of spring flowers are

breaking through the frozen ground.

The first earth worm out for a stroll

was found crawling on the road.

A rescuer put it beside the crocuses.

Signs of the sun make us ready

to work in the garden, which isn't!

A season of growth is about to

awaken after an extended rest.

The spring flowers are a visual

reminder another season has passed.

The idea for raised beds didn't

seem so smart a few years ago.

Now I wonder, why didn't I buy more?

Suitor

Aooo, aooo, aooo,
the desperate mating calls
come from the tall pine.

Silence. Then a short time later,
the calls are repeated.
Why is it three times?

I walk toward trees to identify
the source but I hear it fly off.
At least I know now it's a bird

desperately calling out
in the early morning cold
trying to entice a mate.

I Could Do Without

I could do without
all the dandelions and
creeping Charlie in the yard
or the chipmunks that enjoy the
raspberries as much as we do.

I could do without all
the new gadgets that allow
you to purchase things you used
to be able to try on at the store
before you bought them.

I could do without the
loss of conversation with
our grandkids because of
the thing in their hands
that 'requests' their attention.

I could do without all
the pain my body feels when
I do something physical,
yet I'm glad they are things
that I can still experience.

Travel

Clump, clump,

    everything in the plane

goes up, then down

    with every expansion joint.

The access lanes are

    like some of our roads.

It's a good thing

    we're flying to Seattle.

Evening Wrap

Stick season is over.
Various shades of
green are emerging.

Nature's leaky umbrella
is unfolding while
preparing for new growth.

The moon tries to be
noticed in the fading light
despite thin cloud cover.

The hawks' height in
the air has dipped as
they review the menu.

The robins' brief
serenade before dark
has repetitively begun.

The first mosquito bite
of the season is registered;
time to go inside.

Poetry Festival

Finally, a day with sunshine this early spring.
The old schoolhouse by the brook looked as
inviting as the sign outside: Poetry Festival.

Too bad there were only about a dozen cars
in the parking lot, but that would also make it
a more relaxed setting to enjoy the readings.

A friend had invited me and asked me
to bring some of my poetry to read.
Seeing him again would be worth the trip.

With COVID and a motorcycle accident,
I hadn't seen him in at least two years.
An accomplished writer, but poetry?

Even though the group was small, the
authors didn't disappoint, with thoughts
as varied as the subject matter.

Season of Pleasure

The snow is gone.
The rake feels comfortable,
initially, but I should have taken
the time to find my gloves.

Spring flowers are on display
and taking full advantage.
The onions and garlic are
patiently waiting for company.

Soon their presence will
hardly be noticed, as all
the other vegetables will
claim space in the garden.

Another season of pleasure
learned at a young age
that now requires some
assistance to accomplish.

But who's complaining?

Spring Frost

A blast of summer heat arrives
after a hard, late spring frost.

All—farms with orchards to those
of small fruits—are concerned.

With the lack of rain and now this heat,
damage will be on full display.

It Only Happened
Yesterday

As the plane touched the ground,
a load roar echoed
throughout the airplane.

We were in Hawaii
to refuel before continuing
on to California.

It felt good to stand up.
As we got to the tarmac,
it started to rain.

The rain felt refreshing,
like it was cleansing
us of Vietnam.

It was obvious,
many of us were
having the same thoughts.

We casually walked into
the terminal in a totally
relaxed frame of mind.

A couple of hours later came
the call to re-board. The sun
was shining and so were we.

Forty-nine years later, we flew back.
The memories flooded back as if
it only happened yesterday.

Delivery Truck

A delivery truck stops
in front of our home.

My wife says
"They're here,"

with a bit of a mocking
tone in her voice.

I didn't think I had
been so obvious.

The driver hands me a box.
I carry it inside and

set it down on the counter.
I start to walk away only to

hear, "Well aren't you going
to open your surprise?"

"In a bit," I say, which only
fuels the verbal banter.

I draw a knife from a
drawer to cut the tape.

There in the box are copies
of my newest book.

Even though I spent months
putting it together, it is

rewarding to view a segment
of my life bound together.

The poems are like
a picture in words.

The moment that caused
each poem to be created

is revisited each time
I read the piece.

If it does the same
for others, that is great.

But in a surprising way,
it really doesn't matter

as long as it talks to me.
The moment remains alive.

Move On

The repetitive, monotonous chorus
of the robins is finally dwindling.

The moon, visible in the afternoon
sky, retreated with the sun

leaving the nighttime sky dark
to the delight of the stars.

Bugs drawn by the dim light of the
solar lamps flutter around, drawing

the attention of several hungry bats.
Since you can't always see

the direction they're coming from,
I think I will move on as well.

Bike Day

As families arrive,
excited preschoolers
help their parents with their
scooters, tricycles or bikes.

Today, there will be no one
who comes to the school who
won't be playfully shown
how good they are at riding.

Even if it's the mail man,
he will be expected to
watch and admire, because
today is 'Bike Day.'

Jazz Fest

A crowd has gathered
in front of City Hall in
anticipation of hearing
the junior high band.

When they begin,
toes start tapping.
Bodies begin to sway with
the rhythm of the music.

All their practice pays off.
The applause is genuine.
Before you know it,
the concert comes to an end.

Families join together while
surprised visitors comment,
"What a nice way to start
our day at the Jazz Fest."

Turn South

Like young youthful adults
we climb into the car, not
really knowing where we are
going, or why we're headed south.

A garden nursery catches our eye
so we stop and look around.
Must be too early for tomato plants.
We have enough flowering plants.

We walk back to the car.
I remember someone talking
about an ice cream place
near here, so we continue south.

Not far away, what is left of
a small town comes into view.
A sign saying "creemees and
cookies" catches our eyes.

Now that's two things you're
never too old for, don't you agree?
We join cars from different states
in the crowded parking lot.

We stand in the line to order.
With our treats in hand, we sit at a
picnic table to enjoy our treats.
It was a good decision to turn south.

Distinctive Sunset

The hot summer sun
mixes with the humidity
of recent rains, causing
a brief afternoon storm.

Thunder echoing from
the darkening sky is
enhanced by sporadic
bolts of lightning.

Brief but dramatic,
it disperses in time
to become part of
a distinctive sunset.

Falls Park

Falls Park in Vergennes makes
a nice backdrop for pictures
that exudes history.
What was in this building, or that?

Even though the water was high,
we took out our fishing gear from
the vehicle in the crowded parking lot
to an open spot along the shoreline.

The rain held off long
enough for my sons and
grandchildren to test their
skills on Fathers' Day.

At times, large fish would jump
out of the water below the falls
but don't worry, we weren't
able to gain their attention.

Lost Prestige

The sun is hesitant
to set on this, the
longest day of the year.

Light fluffy clouds
wait to highlight the
sunset as it arrives.

The night will
gradually recover its lost
prestige along the way.

PART II

Ms. Am

"Oh Am. This is so—"

"Can I help you?"

"Yes, backpack heavy—"

"There you are."

"Thank you Ms. Am."

"You are strong girls."

"Yes we are," they say

as the preschool students

head for the door with a smile.

Ms. Am watches with pride.

Let It Fly

Why does sharing
something as personal
as your writing feel like
you're exposing yourself?

Yet many others are
comfortable with
revealing various things
when they create.

No matter what it is,
they let it fly.
Why can't I
do the same?

The books are written.
I just have to accept
modern technology is
the way to connect.

Merlin

We have a new addition
to the trees around our home.

It's not a new songbird
that fed from our feeders.

These birds have in fact been
feeding on those small birds.

They're a rare type of raptor
called Merlin Hawks.

Many of those birds that
we fed all winter are gone.

The morning chorus
has become very limited.

The calls the hawks make
are now easily heard.

They have been able
to feed their family well.

Kind of sad in a way,
yet a fact of nature.

Settle Back

The brief afternoon
storm has passed.

Scattered light, puffy
clouds will soon present

a brief backdrop to
highlight the sunset.

The Merlin Hawk family
has left the tall pine tree.

A robin breaks the silence
with a brief serenade.

The raspberries are picked.
Time to settle back and

take it all in, but as the
sunset fades, so do I.

Help Wanted

A "Help Wanted" sign
hangs in the window
of a downtown store.

Outside the store
is a cardboard-covered
section of sidewalk.

A man and a woman lie
dressed on top with a pillow,
a full shopping cart by them.

It is sad to see how these
people have reduced their
value to garbage can status.

My dad would have asked,
"What's wrong with this picture?"
I simply ask, "Why?"

But This Is Our Home

"You know this is a
public park. You need
to pack up and move."

"But officer, this is our
home. We're taking up
such a small part of it."

"This is temporary.
You know the rules
and you agreed to them."

"But officer, where do we
put our stuff now that we
have to leave our home?"

"You were given bags.
I can't tell you but
you can't leave it here."

With this, the officers
stepped away to
allow several to dress.

They tried not to interfere
as various comments were
made while the group packed up.

Several left behind trash
but one person did pick it up.
Now, no visitors will ever know.

Joint Effort

Our numerous discussions
opened the door to hiring a
professional landscaper for ideas.

After receiving them,
it was obvious we were
not on the same page.

A reboot of our own ideas that
we were both comfortable
with began our joint effort.

As it developed, we
altered our plans when
we felt it was needed.

The plants are no
different than us—they need
to be noticed, yet fit in.

Yep

"What are you doing?" my wife asked.

"Looking out the window," I reply.

"Oh, at what?"

"The steam coming off the road."

"Ah, sounds like you're busy."

"Yep!"

"Are you going to take a break soon?"

"Maybe I'll get something to drink."

"Think you will mow then?"

"Probably."

"Well, that's nice to know."

"Yep. It takes a lot of planning."

Garden Center

On our trip to the garden center, we
have a flexible list as a starting point.

Having both been raised
on family farms in Iowa,

we're comfortable working
with our hands in the dirt.

A special here or a bargain
there usually finds a home.

After all, we find peace working
in the soil that raised us.

Sunny Shower

"Listen, what do you hear?"

"Yes grandpa, I hear it. What is it?"

"Do you hear the rustle of the leaves?"

"Yes, but the wind isn't blowing."

"Could it be rain?"

"No, the sun is shining."

"Look up at the cloud coming toward us."

"How can it be rain if—oh, it's raining!"

"Would you call it a sunny shower?"

"Oh, Grandpa. Did you bring soap?"

"Did you bring towels?"

"Does this mean our weeding is over?"

"I think so."

"Thank you, sunny shower."

The Writer

When you read something
that creates a vision, you
understand why the author
graced the paper with a pen.

Unlike a painter, a writer
tries to record an image in
words that recreate the scene.

They do this for themselves.
If someone else reads it
and has similar feelings,

the writer realizes their
account of the moment was
successfully accomplished.

Connections

Root cuttings from various
day lily varieties that mom planted
to hide the water pump were
planted at each of our homes.

Being raised on a farm,
rhubarb, perennials, even
walnuts came with us to
maintain our memories.

What is within your
home that was a part
of your youth that kept
those connections alive?

Rocking Chair

The rocking chair
is empty, yet rocks
silently on the deck.

It should be still,
but because of
the wind, it's not.

The normal warmth
that would be its
reward is absent,

yet the emptiness
allows it to relax
during this free ride.

Decision

The blazer and pants
hang next to the
dress in the closet.

Both of them fit,
but which will it be
today when I go out?

Do I feel pretty
or do I just want
to be present?

I wish the decision
was that easy,
but it is not.

Kai

He started playing
the piano, then decided
to add the trumpet.

It was fine in the
summer but in the winter,
no place was big enough.

He then added playing soccer
after a friend decided
that he would try it.

He enjoyed it and
soon added events in
track and field.

He placed in the top
five of his age group
for the whole state.

He decided to practice
so he could do it right.
Now he is in the top three.

Even he was surprised.
Now we can't wait
to see what is next.

Let Go

The fishing pole
is in good shape.
The reel is not.

Don't even remember
the last time I
used that pole.

I sure remember
receiving it. A gift
for my tenth birthday.

Complete with a
left-handed reel
that no longer works.

One of those fancy
flip the bar types
before you cast.

You just had to learn
when to take your finger
off the line.

The memories are mine.
Our sons and their families
already have modern gear.

The pile dwindles of things
from the past I might
use again, you just never know.

I'll put the things still useful
in bags for the secondhand
shop, except the pole.

Prepare

It's mid-August but if you
looked at the red maple
in the yard, you'd think
it's mid-September.

There are more red leaves
on the ground than on the tree.
Was it the recent heavy rain
that assisted their descent?

Last night, wild geese flew
over our home, headed South,
honking during the process
to keep everyone together.

The signs nature provides us
are not hard to follow.
We just have to pay
attention and prepare.

Lawn Sale

The tables are set up
for the lawn sale, to hold
the assorted items.

Spurred on by our oldest
grandchild, we start
setting up for the sale.

From clothing to books
to adolescent toys, they
receive lengthy reviews.

Young children discover
this or that while their
parents keep them calm.

A little bit of give
and take allows the
parent to concede.

The once-special items
have found life out of
a box, in a new home.

Robin

There was a robin
by a flower patch I
was preparing to weed.

I started down at
the far end without
disturbing the bird.

It even joined me,
looking for worms where
I had pulled weeds.

Suddenly it flew off as
a young preschooler
ran over to me.

"Did I scare the bird?"
he asked. "Yes, you did,"
I said as his teacher came over.

Robin asked, "Why did
you cross the line without
asking permission to do so?"

Embarrassed, he looked at me.
I said, "You don't want to upset a
bird or your caring teacher."

Glimpse From the Past

As I'm mowing
our lawn with my
riding lawn mower,

two teenage girls
ride by on their bikes.
One is sitting up pedaling

while the other is bent
over the handlebars
trying to gain more speed.

As they head down the hill,
she puts her feet out to
the side to go faster.

Wow, just like I did
when I was a kid
over seventy years ago

much to the displeasure
of my mother—but at least
now they wear helmets.

Cautious Feeling

The cool morning air requires
the use of a sweatshirt.

Soon this will seem warm,
but not this morning.

The forest sounds are alive
with competing voices

as I prepare to work in
the surrounding gardens.

Even though the church
is off a major road,

the road traffic is but
dull background music.

When I get to a section where
poison ivy has returned,

I start to weed between
the black-eyed Su...

What was that sound?
The crow notices it too—

he calls out a warning—
but I see no movement.

There it is again, which
brings another warning call.

Whatever it is, it's big.
So why can't I see it?

A cautious feeling is building.
I pick up my tools and head

for the car. What I have left
can be completed another day.

Nothing to Watch

The light is fading as the
cricket chorus inherits the stage.

The solar deck lights are
drawing intimate attention.

Groups of kids have
parked their assorted bikes.

They will be together again to
board the bus in the morning.

Even a neighbor's pool
is silent this evening.

A whining dog is trying to
convince his owners

to allow him to come inside
since there's nothing to watch.

New Faces

Many of the faces have changed;
there are only a few teachers I know.

The young preschool students are
getting to know one another.

There are times when someone is
vocally unhappy, even in the woods.

Soon, joyful screams replace
the brief moment of insecurity.

All are adjusting together with
the start of the new school year.

Have a Place

The scattered faint cloud cover
is creating a dramatic sunset.

The wind from the approaching
storm will reduce the fading foliage.

A raincoat will be mandatory
for the soccer game tomorrow.

Garden cleanup is almost complete.
Preparations have begun for planting bulbs.

The shelves holding jars of canned
goods have room for the applesauce.

Lawn equipment will soon be
moved to the back of the garage.

The snowblower and snow shovels
will proudly move to the front.

Everything seems to have a place,
no matter the season we are shifting into.

Shelburne Farms

As we enter through the main gate,
we drive down a gravel road that
meanders along a walking trail.

Patches of woods on the left,
a broad hay field to the right.
No sign of structures in sight.

As we round a lazy bend, the first
view of farm buildings shocks us.
It's like we've entered a fantasy.

A huge U-shaped complex includes
a lengthy fence across the front of it
to contain anything let out to wander.

Where did they get the designs,
let alone the materials to build such
an incredible, multi-function barn?

Portions of it appear to be part of a castle.
Other sections seem very functional,
whether for food storage or animal housing.

We learn it currently houses offices, a bakery,
a preschool, a cheese processing area,
a workshop and several animal pens.

The bakery gets our attention first.
Bread, cookies and a bun cause us
to seek out a picnic table to enjoy.

Hunger satisfied, the kids' animal
area finds us all petting animals or at least
trying to entice them to notice us.

Since we don't have any food for them,
we get the message and move on to
the wood working shop, which is closed.

The cheese plant is also closed but
there is someone giving out samples
which means we're stopping at the store.

Back to the car, we head towards
the lakeshore to get out and walk.
With a wet summer, there is less beach.

No problem. We join others drawn
by its beauty along with plenty of seating.
Can't forget the abundance of colorful stones.

A skip the stone contest, that really isn't
much of a contest between father and son,
entices others on the beach to try their hand.

With a multicolored stone safely tucked away
in each of our pockets, the serenity of this
afternoon flows home with us as we leave.

Clear weather provides us with views of Mt. Mansfield
as we drive toward the gate. Camel's Hump comes into
view as we round the bend and drive up to the entrance.

What a special afternoon it has been.
What a wonderful place to share as we
all say thank you to the man in the booth.

Shade Garden

It's early on a fall morning.
Well, not really, but it sure feels like it.

The sun has barely reached the
forest as the school bus drives by.

With the first frost of the season,
the fall flowers will soon fade away.

Bulbs waiting to be planted sit
patiently in the bag by the garden.

Preparations are almost complete
for planting them by the ferns.

This will be a way of drawing attention
to the awakening garden in the Spring.

By the time the ferns stretch out, the
tulips will be getting ready for next year.

The lilac bush will briefly
brighten the shade garden

before leaving it all to the variety
of spirited, free-flowing ferns.

Wagon Ride

A music class for young children
and their mothers was going strong.

Containers were being pulled by mothers
while the children laughed and sang.

One little girl looked at me as I
walked in. "I on wagon ride."

When I asked, "Is there room for me?"
She looked intently at the small container

her mother was pulling across the carpet.
Her look turned sad as she shook her head, no!

How precious that brief moment was—
she didn't even realize it, but I did.

The Blues

The morning has arrived to
go to the hospital for surgery.

Fortunately, I have a good team
of doctors who found them and

there was no delay in scheduling
the outpatient operations.

What they did to get at the tumors,
I couldn't tell because of their location.

One of the staff members asked,
"What type of music do you like?"

I said, "The blues."
"Any special performer?"

"Colin James has a good style."
She hadn't heard of him but

after spelling out his name,
she found several of his works.

When they got done with the
medical procedures, she said,

"Thanks for introducing us
to Colin James. It's always

nice to listen to the music
that patients are tuned in to."

It sure put me in another zone
while they did their work.

Next Project

The woodworking shop hasn't
seen much activity lately.

Don't know why, just don't
seem to have anything pending.

It sure looks like I could start
by cleaning off the workbench.

Wow, some of this wood is scraps
from chairs I made for the grand kids.

It was almost eight years
ago that I made the last one.

She had just turned ten and sat
in it for a number of years.

One of her favorite stuffed toys
occupies her place now, in her room.

Well, whatever the reason I had
for saving it, it's in the throw pile now.

Finally, the tools and scraps
are where they belong.

Now I have the room to make
minor repairs to a couple of things

I have been putting off.
Guess they'll be my next project.

First Snow

The first snow of the season
that requires a shovel arrives
just in time for Thanksgiving.

Fortunately, it came
during the night with a
full sun by daybreak.

This allowed the sun to
warm the blacktop enough
to clear off the driveway.

No excuses for anyone
to be late to the table as
we prepare to celebrate.

Wine Time

With both eyes dilated,
I'm asked to sit
in a waiting area that
has one open chair.

Most of us waiting
have gray hair so we
just sit there waiting
to be called for tests.

More people come but
there are no more seats
so they stand until
a chair opens up.

When it does, someone asks,
"Does anyone have a coin?"
A man stands up and flips
a coin while one calls heads.

Without looking at the coin,
he calls "tails" as the
other person waiting
prepares to sit down.

Laughter bursts out as
another is called, so
everyone now has a seat,
but the banter continues.

One gets up, looks at her
watch and proclaims, "It's
after 4:30, wine time," which
causes several others to agree.

"Jones, is Jones in here?"
"I'll give you $25 to be Jones."
"Wait, I'll give you $30."
The nurse smiles and walks off.

From grandkids to
how far they'd have to
drive home, the topics
are varied and open.

As the group thins,
those left behind
move closer together to
continue the conversation.

It's unanimous—don't accept
an afternoon appointment if you
don't want to drive home in the dark,
especially if it affects wine time.

When the Road

When the road feels foreign,
it's wise to discover why.

Sometimes it's obvious while
other times, we just find our way.

In our youth, we barely notice—
in fact, may even feel emboldened.

But as we age, the methods are
altered as our abilities fluctuate.

Our adjustments to them allow
us to proceed down this winding

road that guides us until we're ready
for the next phase of our journey.

PART III

Colorful Sunrise

The colorful sunrise was
our lone sighting of the sun.

Clouds took over as if
assigned to protect us.

The rain soon followed as
gusts of wind cooled the air.

By nightfall, the soft patter
of the rain became silent.

The transition was complete as
snow brightened up the night.

The morning forecaster had advised,
"Locate your snow shovel for this one."

Christmas Wreaths

The cloudy Sunday morning opened
with thoughts of the kids making
Christmas wreaths—were we ready?

That was quickly replaced with,
What's wrong? My left arm tingled
and I had no strength in my left leg.

As I showered and got dressed, it did
not improve. Instead of going to church,
we went to Urgent Care to find out.

We got to the unit as the kids would
have started working on the wreaths.
Their imaginations make the day.

Instead, I am at the hospital starting
tests in the ER before being admitted.
Not what I had envisioned for the day.

The surprise was the chaos in the
Emergency Room caused by people
who obviously needed other services.

Getting to my room was a total relief.
I actually slept for just over an hour
before the day shift came in for rounds.

I had test after test until they were able
to figure out what happened and then
explain it to us, and what was next.

When that happened, my condition had
improved so they let me go home. As we
drove by the church, I thought of the kids.

Did they have enough material?
Since it had been a couple of days,
the wreaths were probably already up.

Hopefully, there will be pictures
displaying each child's creativity—though
missing the stories of their creations.

The Meaning

The outside Christmas ornaments
are still in a box in the basement.

The Christmas tree arrives tonight
with our youngest son and his daughter.

They will put it up along with
the lights and ornaments in an

effort to make this season of
giving feel as normal as possible.

Things sometimes happen at
times when you least expect them.

Fortunately, our sons have
been available to assist us

during my recovery, reinforcing
the meaning of family.

The Beauty of Innocence

"Do you know what I am going to be?
A mermaid," the little girl proudly said.

"That's right," her mother said. "She
has a swim lesson this afternoon."

The little girl smiled as she walked
around the room moving her arms.

Her mother asked, "And what are
you going to do next week?"

She stopped, looked at her mother
before putting an arm over her head

and started to spin around. "That's
right," her mother nodded. "Ballerina class."

The smile said it all as she started
humming music while she spun, bringing

life to her mother's words while we
were treated to the beauty of innocence.

It's Called What

The Christmas gift list given to
us by our grandchildren appears
written in a foreign language.

What is this stuff? It's called what?
How did you learn about it all?
We ask, and immediately wish we hadn't.

They start explaining about
this app or that app, all of
which we have never heard of.

Then they want to put them on our
phones, but we ask them not to,
because we will never use them.

Just tell us what stores are
carrying the items you want so we
can make this a special Christmas.

Christmas Gift

After hanging up a bird feeder
I got for Christmas, I turn
to leave as a chickadee lands.

It is so close to me that the
air from its flight touches me.
He must have been watching.

While I put my things away,
I come out of the garage
as a cardinal starts to feed.

Whether they're competing with
each other or the squirrels, their
voices add so much to this season.

Party

The trip to the grocery store
is now complete.

The bag is full of
food we will never eat.

We are prepared for the
grandkids to be our guests.

A wonderful way to bring
in the New Year—as long as

they don't expect us to be
awake when the ball drops.

Faint Gift

The cold soft north wind is
creating a small band of snow
from the moisture rising off the
warm waters of Lake Champlain.

The personalized snowflakes
greet the residents who reside
along the southern shores but
dissipate as they leave their source.

Those who live a short distance
away aren't aware of the snow
brightening up their neighbors'
lawns as the new year approaches.

A faint gift from the lake
during this season of giving.
Not so much to cause a problem
but enough to enhance the night.

A New Toy

The preschool teachers were
setting up a new toy on the floor.

Long narrow pieces of wood
were placed on top of squares.

When set up, it looked like a
meandering bridge, an inch off the floor.

Carefully, the first one started to walk out.
The others quickly lined up to follow.

"Be careful. Don't fall off into
the water," a smiling teacher said.

When the teacher saw the problems
they were having walking sideways,

she showed them on the floor how to
move sideways to keep their balance.

That way, none of them would fall
off the 'bridge' and into the water.

The teachers smiled as one said softly, "Isn't
it nice to see the joys a new toy brings?"

Split Level Highway

The pines and the hardwoods are
interspersed in the neighborhood.

To stay out of the deep snow,
the squirrels use the lower

branches of the various pine trees
before ascending up to reach the

branches of the hardwoods, as they
progress towards the various feeders.

To reach our feeders, they have to
walk the top rail of a metal fence.

This means that it is one at a time,
but squirrels aren't always patient,

as the deep holes in the snow
by the fence will verify.

As the winter wears on,
trails by the fence develop

for easier access as they return
the way they came, just slower.

Winter Treat

The night was cold.
The roads were clear.

We were early but there
were few parking spots left—

signs of a large crowd for
the elementary concert.

A night to reveal the results
of hours of practice.

It did not disappoint.
First the string instruments,

then the 4th grade band played.
When the 5th grade band started,

it was amazing to see the growth in
musical ability one year made.

The combined elementary chorus
closed out the eventful evening.

What a wonderful scene, as many
swayed while they sang.

Family and friends swaying in
the audience blended right in.

Hidden

Jokes on local TV about finally seeing a
glimpse of the sun have become common.
Days when you can see across the lake are noted.

Others have given advice to go skiing—
when you get to the top of the lift above the clouds,
unfold a lawn chair to soak up some sun.

Like taking a bad vacation without being
able to see the scenery which you know
is out there but hidden in our midst.

Today the sun is shining for the first time
in almost three months. Whiteface,
Mount Mansfield and Camel's Hump

are boldly flaunting their winter apparel.
The beauty causes locals to stop and
take it in, before the clouds return tomorrow.

Pinecone

The warmth of the sun
along with almost no
snow allows us to rake
pinecones in February.

This is the fourth time this
area has been raked since
last fall as they began falling
from the pines like confetti.

It hasn't been that long
since I started raking, but it
sure doesn't feel like it. A father
and his daughter walk over.

"My daughter was wondering
what you are doing," he says.
I explain, then ask her,
"Would you like a pinecone?"

"Can I?" she asks as her
father nods his head yes.
She picks up a pinecone
and says, "Thank you."

They go to the car to go
home but as they drive by,
she holds her pinecone
high so I am sure to see it.

Penguin Plunge

Inspired by Oakley

Will I
        or will I not?

The ice on the water
        is floating in chunks.

Why would I
        go into the water?

Looking around
        there are people everywhere,

all prepared to do
        what I am questioning.

It's good they are
        going by groups.

I still have time
        to step aside, or...

They look — like they
        are having fun.

Look, they're all laughing—
        some are even swimming.

We're next.
        I think I'll swim.

The Soil That Raised Me

The spring garden catalogs
have started to arrive

months before the ground
even considers cooperating.

Yet they're like a good book
that causes your mind to drift off.

They expose you to new
varieties to consider planting.

Being raised on a farm
before a lot of the modern

equipment was developed,
the soil was our lifeline.

Fresh produce and fruit
came from the garden.

A lot has changed over
the last seventy-five years.

Canning was essential then,
especially for a large family.

Now it is rare to see a garden
capable of feeding a family.

Whether we lived in Iowa,
New York or Vermont,

the ability to get outside in
the soil has been my connection as

life has progressed. The feel
of the soil is natural to me.

It doesn't feel like work.
It's like I'm with a friend.

Whitecaps

We watched the whitecaps boldly dance
across the lake's broad surface as we waited.

When the ferry pulled away from shore,
the strength of the waves took hold.

Several people got out of their vehicles to take
pictures as the wind blew out of the South.

When the ferry turned slightly, the waves
started to strike the ferry broadside, sending

sheets of water up, soaking everything.
Drenched, they rushed back to their cars

before the next wave hit the ferry.
Despite the whitecaps and dramatic

sunset over the mountains, the cold
February ice water was not worth it.

Smiling, I realized, that could have included
me if I had been able to reach my phone.

Back Yard

It's March 1st and the last of
the snow has already melted.

A commotion in the backyard
by the feeders draws my attention.

The yard is full of black birds back
from the South, and they are hungry.

They're driving off the squirrels
to eat the food left on the ground.

By the next day, they are gone
as they proceed on their journey.

Life returns to normal in our back
yard until the next travelers arrive.

My Guide

As the sun fades behind
the mountainous horizon,

the moon is exposed as it
clears the Green Mountains.

The brightness of the moon
enhances the bitter cold evening.

As I line up to wait for the ferry,
the moon seems to be alive,

almost as if I'm a part of it.
How can I explain this?

When in Vietnam, the moon
became like a calendar for me.

When I returned, it has always
been a fixture in my life to check.

My feelings as I sit in my car
are so strong, I question myself.

Was it because of a recent minor stroke,
the moon's history in my life, or is it because

it has been so cloudy this Winter
that I haven't seen it for months.

As I board the ferry, I can't see
the moon because of a semi.

As the ferry shifts direction,
its presence is everywhere.

With the rough water, it is
giving off a pulsating feeling.

When the ferry stops to unload,
I pull off and stop in the lot to

take in the moon one more time
before turning my focus to the road.

When I arrive home, I look up and
say, "Thank you for being my guide."

A New Day

The sun has cleared
the ridge line as it
starts to filter through
the pines and sticks.

Frost on the windshield
betrays the temperature.
Mating calls echo throughout
the trees in the quiet community.

Flashing yellow lights disturb
the setting as children rush out of
their homes while dogs voice their
displeasure at being left behind.

My heavy vest and sweatshirt
feel good this morning as
I fill the bird feeder for one
of the last times this winter.

Got the fishing poles ready
for fishing bullheads early
because of almost no ice and
the unusually warm weather.

I will try and find someone who
also enjoys fishing, since my wife
doesn't want me to go alone, but
doesn't like reading in the cold.

Safe Zones

The sounds of the wetlands,
even in mid-March,
are varied yet unmistakable.

You can tell the locations of
each species as they prepare safe
zones for raising their young.

It is hard to believe this is
already happening as I bait
my hooks and prepare to cast.

The sun is shining but the
breeze off the bay
is relentless, even with a coat.

The fish are cautious, not
as ready to feed as they would be
if the water was warmer.

Any bite is a reward;
any fish in the bucket
will taste good tonight.

Stony Point

The parking lot is empty
except for the boat docks.

A crow stands guard in a tree
as it welcomes me, cluck, cluck.

I find a spot to sit on the small
narrow point that is out of the wind.

Two geese round the point stop,
as if surprised by my presence.

They soon wander away from
the shoreline before moving on.

The wind shifts out of the North
as the waves start to come up

higher onto the rocks of the point.
So much so, I have to move higher.

I see why there is no vegetation.
The lake water keeps this area

barren leaving the veins of the
water worn boulders exposed.

Find a Seat

There isn't much to do
when you drop your car off
for routine maintenance
other than find a seat.

Humility is written over
a wall of windows.
Is that for us who
are patiently waiting?

Passion is over another
section. Can't for the
life of me figure out
how to wait with passion.

Integrity completes the
word game on the wall.
Does that mean it was good
we were all there with our cars?

Tables with chairs and no
television, but there is
a barrel of basketballs
with a basketball hoop.

Two young girls discover
it and start to play, causing
several people to get up
to give them space to react.

If it wasn't so cold out,
I'd walk next door, but
then I'd probably buy
something I don't need.

Light and Fluffy

The snow is light and fluffy
in this first phase of the storm.

This afternoon, the southern phase
will move in, with wet, heavy snow.

The snowblower will come to
life for the second time this winter.

This is great for the ski areas, which
our families are preparing for tomorrow.

For those of us unable to participate,
it revives a lot of great memories.

Boxes

Amazing—look at all these boxes.
Didn't we just do this a few years ago?

Why did we keep so much stuff?
Wow, I can remember buying this.

And there are those warm slippers I
accused my wife of throwing away.

They are really worn out. Guess I'll
throw them before she notices them.

Look at all the ties carefully folded.
Do I even remember how to tie one?

So much is in good condition but just
doesn't meet either of our sons' needs.

It makes me wonder why we box anything
since so much in our lives has changed.

Heavy, Wet Snow

The heavy, wet snow is
testing the strength of the pines,

leaving cotton-candy type
balls on the ends of shrubs.

It's the perfect snow for yard
creations, yet there are none.

The early spring flowers have
been entombed in the snow.

Birds of spring are clustered
together on the ground under shrubs,

voicing their displeasure—or are
they just trying to keep warm?

The warmth of the sun tomorrow
will deplete the evidence, free

the flowers to its glow
and brighten our spirits.

Surprise Find

While at a facility that takes in
various forms of yard waste, I
saw several walnuts on the ground.

Growing up on a farm in the Midwest,
foods that kept all winter without
being processed were essential.

We'd break them open, take the nut out,
then add to salads, cakes, or even
cookies to provide a nutty flavor.

I even brought some back from my
parents' home in Iowa to plant
in our orchard in upstate New York.

Between the deer and squirrels,
I did get several to survive by
way of some protective fencing.

It's amazing how finding something
so unexpectedly can produce all of
these thoughts of food that consume me.

Dance Team

Everyone is seated.
The team walks out onto
the floor to cheers,
then stops, in formation.

As soon as the pulsating
music starts, their bodies
react in unison to the
pounding beat of each note.

Spectators watching can't help
but flow with the music in the
stands as they watch the team
briefly bring life to the song.

My Keys

When you see someone
you haven't seen in a while,

it's amazing how the
memories are reignited.

How good it feels to update each
other as if it was yesterday.

Even though our
hair is gray and our

bodies move differently,
our spirits are lifted.

Makes us feel younger
even though we are

now talking about the
children of our children,

complete with pictures
and heartwarming stories.

How can we ever forget?
Now, where did I put my keys?

The Eclipse

The Nor'easter has
overstayed its welcome.

Four days of rain
and snow is enough.

The moment of interest
will soon be upon us.

Millions have planned
for this occasion.

They booked rooms over
a year ago when the path

of the total eclipse of the
moon and the sun was released.

Being within that path of totality,
what have we done to prepare?

We have shoveled some snow,
then let the rain finish it.

Went and found our lawn chairs
and got our solar eclipse glasses.

Now we just need this storm
to take up a new residence.

It Happened

The morning sun brought
smiles to our faces.

The forecast confirmed we
were going to see the eclipse.

Our daughter-in-law had been
busy planning for months.

As I dug out the lawn chairs
and set up a table, we were ready.

We took our positions in
our driveway to observe.

Initially, it didn't appear
much was happening.

Then we put on our solar
glasses. There were no words.

Finches and chickadees became
vocal, then the robins.

About then the mosquitoes came
out of nowhere, with a purpose.

When it reached total eclipse,
the solar driveway light came on.

The sky became a grayish blue,
the breeze stopped, and it got cold.

As the sun started to break free,
nature began to recover.

It began to warm up again.
Couldn't help but feel humbled

for what we had just witnessed
—and accept our status in nature.

AUTHOR NOTES

The birds of spring are celebrating their arrival. The soil has started to soften in places. The first earth worms have reached the fresh air. The flower bed is being highlighted by areas of green. It's the time of year I reach a comfortable level as if I am also coming to life.

Whether we lived in Iowa, upstate New York or Vermont, it was a time of preparing for the window of growth. There were things that you couldn't prepare for like a late frost that would devastate some fruit varieties but there was always a lot you could do that would increase the rewards throughout the summer and fall. As we were canning or freezing, it was such a reward for all the long hours and time we spent working with the soil. It was like soul food for the body.

I thought this would be my last book of poetry. My body told me something was wrong so I went to see my doctor. There was and after surgery, I am in the recovery phase. Hopefully I will be able to continue to connect with my garden at home and a church we attend. There is a preschool there and the children love learning about the flowers. Sometimes they give me more credit than I deserve, but who's complaining? Hopefully the exposure to the soil and its beauty will be passed on to some of the next generation.

ABOUT THE AUTHOR

Roger Watters was born and raised in rural Iowa on a family farm. The very lifestyle helped form his bond with nature throughout his life. Poetry was a form of expression he became comfortable with after returning from Vietnam. *"From the Avenues of the Mind"* was his first book followed by *"Toothpick Forest"*, *"Stationary Witness"*, *"Who Stayed"*, *"Voice of My Pen"* and *"Simple Thoughts."* Several close friends called him, (a common man's poet) after his third book because his work was easy to relate to. Roger has also written a book of short stories titled *"A Picture of Life"* and a book about the formation and history of a fishing and hunting club he was a member of. *"Diamond Faces—The Story of Diamond Sportsmen's Club"* available through the club in South Colton, New York.